She Persisted

VIRGINIA APGAR

—INSPIRED BY—

She Persisted

by Chelsea Clinton & Alexandra Boiger

. . . .

VIRGINIA APGAR

. . . .

Written by
Dr. Sayantani DasGupta

Interior illustrations by
Gillian Flint

PHILOMEL

PHILOMEL BOOKS
An imprint of Penguin Random House LLC, New York

First published in the United States of America by Philomel,
an imprint of Penguin Random House LLC, 2021.

Visit us online at penguinrandomhouse.com.

Library of Congress Cataloging-in-Publication Data

Names: DasGupta, Sayantani, author. | Flint, Gillian, illustrator.
Title: She persisted : Virginia Apgar / written by Dr. Sayantani DasGupta; interior illustrations by Gillian Flint.
Other titles: Virginia Apgar
Description: New York : Philomel Books, 2021. | Series: She persisted | Includes bibliographical references. | Audience: Ages 6–9 | Audience: Grades 2–3 | Summary: "A biography of Virginia Apgar in the She Persisted series"—Provided by publisher.
Identifiers: LCCN 2020047612 | ISBN 9780593115770 (hardcover) | ISBN 9780593115787 (paperback) | ISBN 9780593115794 (ebook)
Subjects: LCSH: Apgar, Virginia, 1909-1974—Juvenile literature. | Anesthesiologists—United States—Biography—Juvenile literature. | Women physicians—United States—Biography—Juvenile literature. | Physicians—United States—Biography.
Classification: LCC RD80.62.A64 D37 2021 | DDC 617.9/6092 [B]—dc23
LC record available at https://lccn.loc.gov/2020047612

Printed in the United States of America

HC ISBN 9780593115770
PB ISBN 9780593115787

10 9 8 7 6 5 4 3 2 1

Edited by Jill Santopolo.
Design by Ellice M. Lee.
Text set in LTC Kennerley.

The publisher does not have any control over and does not assume any responsibility for author or third-party websites or their content.

To my fellow woman physician writers,
we who live at the intersection of
the stethoscope and the pen.

She
Persisted

....

Dear Reader,

As Sally Ride and Marian Wright Edelman both powerfully said, "You can't be what you can't see." When Sally Ride said that, she meant that it was hard to dream of being an astronaut, like she was, or a doctor or an athlete or anything at all if you didn't see someone like you who already had lived that dream. She especially was talking about seeing women in jobs that historically were held by men.

I wrote the first *She Persisted* and the books that came after it because I wanted young girls—and children of all genders—to see women who worked hard to live their dreams. And I wanted all of us to see examples of persistence in the face of different challenges to help inspire us in our own lives.

I'm so thrilled now to partner with a sisterhood of writers to bring longer, more in-depth versions of these stories of women's persistence and achievement to readers. I hope you enjoy these chapter books as much as I do and find them inspiring and empowering.

And remember: If anyone ever tells you no, if anyone ever says your voice isn't important or your dreams are too big, remember these women. They persisted and so should you.

Warmly,
Chelsea Clinton

VIRGINIA APGAR

TABLE OF CONTENTS

....

· ·

A Busy Bee

Virginia "Ginnie" Apgar was born on June 7, 1909, in Westfield, New Jersey, into a family that, in her own words, "never sat down." This go-go-go quality would define the rest of her amazing life.

Virginia's father, Charles Apgar, was a salesman—of cars and insurance. But Charles's real love was inventing things. He spent hours doing experiments on radio waves with his wireless telegraph and building his own telescope in his basement laboratory. He also taught Virginia to read when she was only three years old. Reading was a family passion for the Apgars, as was music. Virginia started taking violin lessons when she was six, and she and her older brother Lawrence played family concerts with their parents.

Due to Charles often changing jobs, the Apgar family was not very well off. They lived modestly, and sometimes had to take paying lodgers who rented rooms in their home to make ends meet. Yet, as a family friend once noted, "[The family had] the respect . . . of all who know them."

Even though Virginia never met a woman physician when she was young, she knew she wanted to study medicine from a very early age. Her friend Joan Beck remembers, "She always told interviewers she couldn't remember a time in her life when she wasn't intent on going into medicine." Maybe she was inspired by her father's amateur scientific work. Maybe she was motivated by the stories she heard about her eldest brother, who died from a disease called tuberculosis before she was born. Or maybe she was inspired by her older brother Lawrence, who suffered from chronic eczema, an itchy skin condition that needed many doctor appointments throughout his life.

Virginia's busy high school schedule shows

that her life as a fast talker, fast thinker and fast mover started early on. One of her senior yearbook quotes reads, "Time was precious to her and her mind and hands were never still." Virginia was a member of the orchestra, debate club, basketball team, tennis and track teams. She collected stamps, taught herself Greek and was interested in higher mathematics. She was an excellent science student, but didn't do well in home economics—a class that many high schoolers, especially girls, used to have to take to learn cooking, cleaning, ironing and sewing. Supposedly, Virginia never learned to cook, and later in her life, she would be quoted as saying that she never married because "I haven't found a man who can cook."

In her yearbook, next to her senior picture, another quote reads "The industry of the bee is second only to that of Virginia . . . Frankly, how does she do it?" And guess who, in the class catalogue, was elected "most studious"? That's right! Our own Ginnie Apgar!

ustry
.he bee
Virginia

One of Nine

After high school, Virginia attended Mount Holyoke, an all-women's college on a beautiful wooded Massachusetts campus. Other famous women went to Mount Holyoke, too, including poet Emily Dickinson and Frances Perkins, the first woman appointed to a presidential cabinet. A lot of women who went to Mount Holyoke had families who were able to pay their tuition easily. Virginia's family didn't have enough money to send her to college, but she persisted in trying to get herself there and was lucky enough to be able to make it happen. She convinced two Westfield women to give her loans, and won some scholarship money so she could attend college. She also worked many jobs in college, opening the school library every morning, waiting tables, cleaning the anatomy laboratory, and more. Virginia Apgar never stopped!

In addition to all this, she also played violin in the Mount Holyoke orchestra, reported for the college newspaper, acted in dramas and was a member of eleven athletic and academic teams and seven varsity teams. She majored in zoology—the study of different animal species and their behavior—and minored in other scientific fields. Her zoology professor and adviser once said that it was rare to find

a student so engaged with her subject and "with such a wide knowledge of it."

In September of 1929, after graduating from Mount Holyoke, Virginia Apgar went to New York City for medical school. She became a student at Columbia University College of Physicians and Surgeons (also known as P&S) just before the crash of the stock market, which was a system where many people—including Virginia's family—invested a lot of their money. The Apgars lost much of the savings they had. In 1929 a family friend wrote a letter to Columbia University's scholarship committee to help Virginia, explaining her need for scholarship money. In the letter, he noted that Mr. Apgar had changed jobs a lot and had not been able to save enough for Virginia's medical school fees. The man also wrote that because of her "energy, ability, application and interest" Virginia would deserve any money she received. Even the stock market crash couldn't stop Virginia.

But something else could have stopped her: the fact that she was a woman. It was not very easy for American women doctors at the time. The first American woman to graduate medical school, Elizabeth Blackwell, got her medical degree in 1849, after many rejections and struggles. This was at a time when women were considered unfit to practice medicine, just because they were women! Because of the persistence of those early women doctors and medical students, though, seventeen women's medical schools and nine women's hospitals were founded between 1848 and 1895, and more women became physicians over these years too. Unfortunately, a number of these women's medical institutions closed after 1910, and between 1910 and 1945, there were fewer women doctors with fewer chances to practice medicine. When Virginia Apgar entered medical school, she was one of only nine woman medical students in her class, compared with dozens of men.

But Virginia didn't let being one of a few women in medical training slow her down, or make her unfeeling to others. Dr. Vera Joseph, who graduated from P&S in 1936, remembers Virginia Apgar in her student days as "a warm, responsive human being." Dr. Joseph, who was of Jamaican and Chinese heritage and one of the first women of color to attend Columbia University College of Physicians and Surgeons, remembers:

When I entered P&S, anxious and uncertain . . . Virginia was a senior and in her keen, perceptive way recognized immediately my need for reassurance and a need for belonging. Virginia was always in motion! A whirlwind of white coat flying through the door of the Women Students Lounge . . . was Virginia entering or leaving on a mission. She never dawdled but she could pause for a cheerful greeting, a reassuring hug, conversation, when needed, for me.

Virginia's "whirlwind" ways had already become a part of her legend in medical school, but she didn't let her high energy or ambitious nature interfere with her being a kind friend.

CHAPTER 3
....

Twice as Good

Virginia Apgar dreamed of becoming a surgeon. After graduating medical school
near the top of her class in 1933, she got a spot
in the very competitive surgical training program
at Presbyterian Hospital in New York City. After
two years of training, though, the Chief of the
Surgical Service, Dr. Allen Whipple, advised her
not to continue in the program, even though she
was doing good work. According to some, he was

worried that Virginia wouldn't be able to make a living as a surgeon, because many patients did not want to get treated by women. Other people suggest this was simply Dr. Whipple being unfair to her because she was a woman.

Allen Whipple encouraged Virginia to switch to anesthesiology—a field involving giving patients medicine so that they fall asleep or do not feel pain during surgeries—a fairly new area that was mostly staffed by nurses, almost all of whom were women. Whipple might have urged her to take this path because he felt it was more "feminine" and therefore "suitable" for a woman. Even though switching specialties was a risk, Virginia decided to take Whipple's advice.

Virginia didn't like to talk publicly about sexism in medicine, but this was clearly one of those times that being a woman stopped her from reaching a dream. Still, Virginia did what she had done and would continue to do when life put stumbling blocks in her path: if she couldn't find a way around them, she would start marching down a brand-new path. When she was later asked if she had ever felt discriminated against as a woman in medicine, she said, "Not at all. If you're a woman, you just have to be twice as good and work twice as hard." But in private conversations and in her diary, Virginia was outraged about things like salary differences between her and her male colleagues (they made more money!) and "stag" (male-only) dinners that often followed doctors' meetings.

Dr. Virginia Apgar left her surgical training program and trained to be an anesthesiologist in New York and Wisconsin. In 1938, she was hired to

teach at P&S, where she eventually became the first woman ever to hold full professorship at Columbia University College of Physicians and Surgeons.

As director of the Division of Anesthesiology, Virginia started a training program to build a full-time staff of doctor-anesthesiologists. She had little funding, had no office, and had no place to stay in the hospital when she was there overnight like doctors who were men did, so she had to pay out of her own pocket for a place to stay in the hospital. In a letter to her former mentor from Wisconsin, Virginia wrote about her frustration: "By the second week, I was ready to turn to law, or dress making." Virginia Apgar continued to dream of leading a department of anesthesiology that would stand on its own, not be a division under surgery. But when she finally was able to turn the division into a full-fledged department in 1949, a man was unfairly made chair of the department instead of her.

Since she wasn't running the department, Virginia changed her focus to obstetrical anesthesia, which meant she treated mothers delivering babies. She also concentrated more on her students, becoming an energetic teacher of medical students who gave fast, information-filled lectures. "She took a sincere personal interest in every one of her students so that they almost always did well because they didn't have the heart to disappoint her," said one of her students. Another student, Dr. L. Stanley James, who later became her colleague, remembers her bubbly and warm personality that "engulfed you. She was one person the medical students never forgot."

Virginia always visited patients the night before
she was to give them anesthesia, reassuring them
with her warm, confident personality, and sometimes telling a joke or two. Her intelligence and
skill were so respected that Columbia staff members always insisted that she be the anesthesiologist

whenever they or their family members needed surgery or were giving birth.

Of course, the best teachers are always learning themselves. According to L. Stanley James: "Learning was the focal point of her life. Her curiosity was insatiable . . . She never became rigid. This rare quality enabled her to progress through life, without becoming walled in by tradition or custom." It was this personality trait that helped Virginia Apgar develop her groundbreaking scale that improved the lives of newborns forever.

....

Making History

D r. Apgar was a keen observer, and as she cared for pregnant and delivering mothers, she found herself noticing something very strange. Even though babies in the U.S. were healthier than they had been in earlier years, many newborns still got sick and died within a day of being born. Part of the problem, Virginia realized, was that babies were going home with health problems that no one had spotted. There was no single standard way that newborn babies were being evaluated, or checked, after birth, and this is the area where Dr. Virginia Apgar would change medicine, and the world, forever.

It started in 1949, over breakfast in the hospital cafeteria. A medical student asked a question about evaluating newborn babies, and Virginia answered, "That's easy, you'd do it like this." The

story goes that she grabbed the nearest piece of paper, a slip that asked people to bus their own trays, and wrote down the five points of what became the Apgar score—the five things to look for to determine a newborn baby's health—before rushing off to the patient floors to try it out. She published her idea for the score in 1953.

The five aspects of infant health were each given a number on a scale of 0–2 with the higher number showing a baby's better health. The evaluation was (and continues to be) done at one and five minutes after birth. Even though Virginia Apgar did not herself use her last name as a way to remember these five qualities of newborn health, eventually some other doctors used the letters of her last name as a way to remember the Apgar score:

Appearance (skin color)

Pulse (heart rate)

Grimace (reflex irritability)

Activity (muscle tone)

Respiration (breathing)

If you're reading this book, and were born in a hospital, it is very likely that a doctor or nurse evaluated YOU when you were one and five min-utes old for all five of these things:

1. Your skin color (Did it look healthy? Were you getting enough oxygen?)

2. Your heart rate (Was it too slow? Too fast?)

3. Your reflexes (If they made a dropping motion with your arms, did you startle and cry?)

4. Your muscle tone (Were you moving your arms and legs strongly?)

5. Your breathing (Was it even, or ragged?)

If your family has the papers they sent you home with, you probably can find out what Apgar scores you got!

Even as Virginia Apgar was making history in her lifetime by inventing and evaluating her newborn scoring system, she was becoming legendary in medical history too. She was a larger-than-life character with a quick mind and a wicked sense of humor. She apparently carried surgical resuscitation equipment—medical tools to help people start breathing—on her at all times, in case she spotted any medical emergencies. She is noted to have once said, "Nobody, but nobody, is going to stop breathing on me!"

In the words of one doctor who was her student, "We remember her best for her unremitting good cheer, her energy, her great enthusiasm for her subject." When she was teaching students about helium, for instance, she would regularly take a few breaths of the gas herself and then lecture her students in a "high-pitched squeak."

"Whenever Virginia was expected at our house," said Virginia's friend Joan Beck, who co-wrote a book with Virginia called *Is My Baby All Right?* "my teenage son and his friends would spend half a day in the library, concocting difficult questions to spring on her. She never failed to get the answers right." Virginia Apgar never spoke slowly, and some remember seeing her have two conversations at the same time on two separate phones, one in each ear. The Columbia University College of Physicians and Surgeons medical class of 1943 had a song about her in their class show (sung to the tune of "Yankee Doodle Dandy"):

The only advice that I can give
If you can get the knack
Is talk as fast as I do
So nobody can talk back.

But I maintain they're wrong.

'Cause I can tell them twice as much

And take only half as long!

Virginia Apgar was not only fast-talking, fast-moving and fast-thinking, but funny, bubbly and brilliant. Although she is remembered for creating the Apgar score worldwide, she is equally remembered by her students and colleagues for her unforgettable teaching style and bedside personality.

....

CHAPTER 5

Marching Forward

Virginia Apgar was not just famous for her contributions to medicine, but to music too. In 1956, Virginia had become friends with a patient named Carleen Hutchins, a high school science teacher and musician who made stringed instruments in her home. Hutchins had one of her self-made violas with her when she was in the hospital for her surgery. In her words, "After the checkup, [Dr. Apgar] played the viola in my room, much to the delight of the whole floor!"

Virginia loved the sound of the instrument so much, she began to learn about instrument making from Hutchins. Working between midnight and

two a.m. in her small apartment bedroom, which was stuffed with woodworking tools and a workbench, Virginia eventually made four stringed instruments—a violin, mezzo violin, cello, and viola. We can imagine how angry her sleeping neighbors might have been at all this nighttime sawing and hammering!

The most famous story about her instrument making is the "phone booth caper." Virginia Apgar and Carleen Hutchins found a piece of curly maple wood perfect for the back of the viola Virginia was making. The only problem was that the wood was the shelf in a pay telephone booth in the lobby of the Harkness Pavilion, a building in the Columbia-Presbyterian Medical Center. Since the hospital refused to give them the shelf, the two decided to steal and replace it!

First, Virginia made a replacement shelf, matching the stain perfectly with the phone booth wood. Under cover of night, the two women took tools to the hospital in a suitcase and Carleen began her work in the phone booth, with Virginia standing guard in the hall in her hospital uniform. Unfortunately, the replacement shelf turned out to be a bit too long, and Carleen had to saw it down to size in the women's restroom. When a passing nurse asked about the noise, Virginia told her, "It's the only time repairmen can work in there."

By the late 1950s Virginia Apgar had attended over 17,000 births. In 1958, she took a year off from her exhausting work at Columbia University ("all babies are born at night" she is known to have said) and went to Johns Hopkins University in Baltimore, Maryland, to study statistics—how numbers and data can be analyzed and understood. Dr. Virginia Apgar earned her degree on her fiftieth birthday, saying, "It was the most difficult thing I ever did."

While at Johns Hopkins, Virginia became more interested in birth defects and how they might be prevented. The infectious disease polio—which could paralyze or kill children—had just been mostly wiped out in the United States because of the polio vaccine, and the National Foundation (also called the March of Dimes) was expanding their work beyond polio to other childhood illnesses and disabilities. The March of Dimes had been founded around World War II by President Franklin D. Roosevelt, who himself had a disability and was a wheelchair user after contracting childhood polio. The organization asked

Dr. Apgar to head their division of birth defects and she accepted. Virginia traveled thousands of miles each year to talk about the importance of early detection (spotting) of birth defects, and the need for more research.

Virginia Apgar spent about fifteen years in different jobs with the March of Dimes. After a terrible epidemic of the infectious disease rubella in 1964 and 1965 caused thousands of babies to die or develop birth defects, she started March of Dimes programs that would help people stop themselves and their babies from getting rubella. She wanted to not just teach people, but also to remove the stigma of birth defects—in other words, she didn't think that the disabilities babies might have should be shameful secrets.

During this time, Virginia still kept up her

hobbies, like gardening and traveling with her violin to play in amateur chamber music quartets in the cities she would visit. At age fifty-nine, she began to take flying lessons, saying that she wanted to be able to fly a plane under the George Washington Bridge!

Virginia became a clinical professor of pediatrics at Cornell University medical school, where she taught teratology (the study of birth defects). She was the first person to hold a faculty position in this new area of study. In 1973, she also became a lecturer in medical genetics at Johns Hopkins University School of Public Health. Virginia Apgar never retired, and while she may have slowed down a little as she got older, she stayed active until her death.

....

CHAPTER 6

Touching the Lives of Millions

At a time when fetal monitors—machines that check on fetuses inside a parent's uterus—had not yet been invented and babies were given little medical attention directly after birth, Virginia Apgar recognized newborns' needs as patients in their own right, and she was the first doctor to treat them that way. She helped begin the fields of neonatology (newborn pediatrics) and established ways for neonatal intensive care units

(NICUs) to provide specialized care to newborn babies.

During her lifetime, Virginia published over sixty scientific articles, as well as many shorter essays for newspapers and magazines, and she received many awards, including honorary doctorates from the Woman's Medical College of Pennsylvania in 1964 and Mount Holyoke in 1965. In 1973, she was elected woman of the year in science by *Ladies' Home Journal*.

Dr. Apgar died on August 7, 1974, at Columbia-Presbyterian, at age sixty-five. In 1994, due to the hard work of champions like Dr. L. Joseph Butterfield of Colorado, Dr. Virginia Apgar was commemorated on a U.S. postage stamp, an appropriate tribute to the lifelong stamp collector. She was inducted into the National Women's Hall of Fame in 1995.

Dr. Apgar touched the lives of millions of babies and families. She also inspired women to pursue careers in medicine, both during her life— when she would give talks encouraging young women to become doctors—and after her death. Dr. Selma Harrison Calmes became an anesthesiologist in the 1960s after reading an essay by Dr. Apgar saying that anesthesiology was a good profession for women with children. Since that time, she has written a lot about Dr. Apgar. Dr. Harrison Calmes notes the importance of "telling the stories of early women doctors. . . . My work on Dr. Virginia Apgar has been especially important to me. Apgar in public denied that being female affected her professional life. But, it was a critical factor, and I was able to document that."

In his eulogy at Virginia Apgar's memorial service at Riverside Church in New York City, pediatrician Dr. L. Stanley James said, "Virginia Apgar is one of the most remarkable people I have ever known. With her, life was exciting. . . . She was warm and compassionate, and at the same time had a great sense of humor. . . . Integrity was her hallmark: she was utterly sincere and honest. . . . And despite her many talents and achievements, she had great humility."

On June 7, 2018, what would have been Virginia Apgar's 109th birthday, she was honored with a Google Doodle. The quartet of instruments she made are still housed at Columbia University

College of Physicians and Surgeons, where they have been played at public events honoring Dr. Apgar. And to this day, whenever a baby is born in a hospital in this country—and in other countries around the world—at one minute and five minutes after they're born, they are given the Apgar score so doctors can make sure they're healthy. In other words, as noted by the U.S. National Library of Medicine, "every baby born in a modern hospital anywhere in the world is looked at first through the eyes of Dr. Virginia Apgar." All babies who have been given the Apgar score are lucky that Dr. Apgar persisted—talking quickly, thinking quickly and chasing her dreams no matter what.

HOW YOU CAN PERSIST

by Dr. Sayantani DasGupta

If you would like to honor Virginia Apgar's legacy, here are some things you can do:

1. Ask your family if they know your Apgar score and if they have the papers from when you were born for you to look at. (You might find your own very small footprint on that paper!)

2. Help a local family with a newborn by offering to play with older children or taking the family dog for a walk!

3. Be kind to someone who might need a listening ear or a supportive friend.

4. Learn about instrument making—or learn how to play a musical instrument.

5. Learn about stamps—including the one honoring Virginia Apgar. Start your own stamp collection, or join a local stamp-collecting club!

6. Tell people about Dr. Virginia Apgar and other pioneering women doctors.

ACKNOWLEDGMENTS

Virginia Apgar persisted in her goals despite many setbacks, but she was not alone. She was supported by friends, family, teachers, benefactors, colleagues and patients. In writing her biography, I have been similarly supported by networks of wonderful people I am honored to acknowledge and thank. Thank you to my agent Brent Taylor, and his colleague Uwe Stender, for encouraging me to write Virginia's story. Thank you to the wonderful editorial team of Jill Santopolo and Talia Benamy at Penguin Random House—it was a joy to work with you! Thank you to Shanta Newlin, as well as the marketing, publicity and copyediting teams who worked on this book. And to the wonderful artists Alexandra Boiger and Gillian Flint and art director Ellice Lee, many thanks for illustrating Virginia's story so beautifully! Much gratitude as well to Chelsea Clinton for envisioning and writing the original She Persisted books to share women's accomplishments with young readers of all genders!

Thank you to the archival librarians at Columbia University Irving Medical Center, who were invaluable to my research into Dr. Virginia Apgar's life, in particular Stephen E. Novak, head of Archives and Special Collections at the Augustus C. Long Health Sciences Library. Thank you to my We Need Diverse Books, Kidlit Writers of Color and Desi Writers families for all the work you do supporting authors of color. Thank you to my pediatrics, narrative-medicine and health-humanities mentors, colleagues and students for always reminding me that science needs good stories, and that stories are good medicine.

Thank you to the teachers, librarians, booksellers and readers who have read my Kiranmala stories and who will read and share

Virginia's story as well. Thank you to my dear family—my parents Sujan and Shamita, my husband Boris, and my darlings Kirin, Sunaya and Khushi—for all the love and support. And thank you to all the women physicians who came before and who will come after me— all of you working to make health care and medicine more accessible, more equitable and more just.

❧ *References* ❧

Beck, Joan. "Virginia Apgar in Memorium."
Clinical Perinatology. Edited by S. Aladjem and
A. K. Brown. St Louis: CV Mosby and Co.,
1974.

Blakemore, Erin. "The Doctor Who Saved
Countless Newborn Babies." *Time*. August 29,
2016. Accessed March 1, 2020. https://time
.com/4460720/virginia-apgar.

Brand, Leonard. "Virginia Apgar in Memorium." *Columbia P&S Quarterly*. Winter 1975, vol. 20 no. 1, p. 27, 30.

Brody, Stacy. "Rise, Serve, Lead! Celebrating Virginia Apgar." *Circulating Now: From the Historical Collections of the National Library of Medicine*. Accessed March 1, 2020. https://circulatingnow.nlm.nih.gov/2019/03/21/rise-serve-lead-celebrating-virginia-apgar.

Brown, Elicia. "Vera Joseph Scholarship Program for Women in Science." Barnard College Website. October 1, 2010. Accessed March 1, 2020. https://barnard.edu/headlines/vera-joseph-scholarship-program-women-science.

Calmes, Selma Harrison. "Apgar and Anesthesiology: A Woman Physician's Career in a Developing Specialty." Prepublished draft from Columbia University Irving Medical Center Archives, eventually published in *Journal of the American Medical Women's Association*. Vol. 39 no. 6.

Calmes, Selma H. "Dr. Virginia Apgar and the Apgar Score: How the Apgar Score Came to Be." *Anesthesia and Analgesia*. May 2015, vol. 120 issue 5, pp. 1060–1064.

Calmes, Selma Harrison. "Virginia Apgar: A Woman Physician's Career in a Developing Specialty." *Journal of the American Medical Women's Association*. Vol. 39 no. 6, p. 184.

Calmes, Selma Harrison. "Virginia Apgar, MD: At the Forefront of Obstetric Anesthesia." *American Society of Anesthesiologists Newsletter.* October 1992, vol. 56 no. 10, p. 9.

Calmes, Selma H. "Virginia Apgar MD Inducted into National Women's Hall of Fame." *American Society of Anesthesiologists Newsletter.* December 1995, vol. 59 no. 12.

Deitrich, B. Letter dated April 30, 1929, to Chas. C. Lieb, MD, Secretary, Committee on Scholarships. From the Columbia University Irving Medical Center Archives. Accessed December 6, 2019.

Enochs, Bonita Eaton. "Virginia Apgar: A Legend Becomes a Postage Stamp. *Columbia P&S Magazine.* Fall 1994.

Google Doodle. Dr. Virginia Apgar's 109th Birthday. Accessed March 1, 2020. https://www.google.com/doodles/dr-virginia-apgars-109th-birthday.

Hunt, Marion. *Days to Remember: A Perennial Calendar: Dedicated to the Life and Times of Virginia Apgar.* New York: Columbia University Health Sciences, 2002.

James, L. Stanley. Eulogy of Virginia Apgar delivered at the Riverside Church in NYC on September 15, 1974. National Library of

Medicine. https://profiles
.nlm.nih.gov/spotlight/cp/catalog
/nlm:nlmuid-101584647X48-doc.

Khalsa, Sita. "Elizabeth Blackwell, MD: America's
First Female Doctor. Amazing Women in
History. October 31, 2012. Accessed March 1,
2020. https://amazingwomeninhistory.com
/elizabeth-blackwell-first-female-doctor.

"Notable Alumnae." Mount Holyoke College
Website. Accessed March 1, 2020. https://
www.mtholyoke.edu/about/notable
/alumnae-changemakers.

Rose, David. "The History of the March of
Dimes." March of Dimes Archives. August 26,

2010. Accessed March 1, 2020. https://www
.marchofdimes.org/mission/a-history-of-the
-march-of-dimes.aspx.

Rose, David. "Virginia Apgar." March of Dimes
Archives. May 28, 2009. Accessed March 1,
2020. https://www.marchofdimes.org/mission
/virginia-apgar.aspx.

Sommerlad, Joe. "Virginia Apgar: Google Doodle
Celebrates the Doctor Whose Simple Health
Test Is Still Saving Newborns Today." *The
Independent.* June 7, 2018.

Sullivan, Walter. "Confession of a Musical Shelf
Robber." *The New York Times.* Feb. 2, 1975.

The Virginia Apgar Papers. National Library of Medicine. Accessed March 1, 2020. https://profiles.nlm.nih.gov/ps/retrieve/Narrative/CP/p-nid/178.

The Weather Vane. Westfield New Jersey High School Yearbook, 1925. Accessed March 1, 2020. http://www.digifind-it.com/westfield/data/yearbooks/1925.pdf.

Yeung, Jessie. "Virginia Apgar's Test Has Saved Millions of Babies: Google Doodle Says Thank You." *CNN Health.* June 7, 2018. Accessed March 1, 2020. https://www.cnn.com/2018/06/07/health/virginia-apgar-intl/index.html.

DR. SAYANTANI DASGUPTA is the *New York Times* bestselling author of the critically acclaimed Bengali folktale–inspired and string theory–inspired Kiranmala and the Kingdom Beyond books, the first of which—*The Serpent's Secret*—was a Bank Street Best Book of the Year, a *Booklist* Best Middle Grade Novel of the 21st Century, and an EB White Read Aloud Honor Book. Sayantani is a pediatrician by training, but now teaches at Columbia University. When she's not writing or reading, Sayantani spends time watching cooking shows with her trilingual children and protecting her black Labrador retriever, Khushi, from the many things that scare him, including plastic bags. She is a team member of We Need Diverse Books.

You can visit Sayantani DasGupta online at
sayantanidasgupta.com
or follow her on Twitter
@sayantani16

GILLIAN FLINT has worked as a professional illustrator since earning an animation and illustration degree in 2003. Her work has since been published in the UK, USA and Australia. In her spare time, Gillian enjoys reading, spending time with her family and puttering about in the garden on sunny days. She lives in the northwest of England.

You can visit Gillian Flint online at
gillianflint.com
or follow her on Twitter
@GillianFlint
and on Instagram
@gillianflint_illustration

CHELSEA CLINTON is the author of the #1 *New York Times* bestseller *She Persisted: 13 American Women Who Changed the World; She Persisted Around the World: 13 Women Who Changed History; She Persisted in Sports: American Olympians Who Changed the Game; Don't Let Them Disappear: 12 Endangered Species Across the Globe; It's Your World: Get Informed, Get Inspired & Get Going!; Start Now!: You Can Make a Difference;* with Hillary Clinton, *Grandma's Gardens* and *Gutsy Women;* and, with Devi Sridhar, *Governing Global Health: Who Runs the World and Why?* She is also the Vice Chair of the Clinton Foundation, where she works on many initiatives, including those that help empower the next generation of leaders. She lives in New York City with her husband, Marc, their children and their dog, Soren.

Courtesy of the author

You can follow Chelsea Clinton on Twitter
@ChelseaClinton
or on Facebook at
facebook.com/chelseaclinton

ALEXANDRA BOIGER has illustrated nearly twenty picture books, including the She Persisted books by Chelsea Clinton; the popular Tallulah series by Marilyn Singer; and the Max and Marla books, which she also wrote. Originally from Munich, Germany, she now lives outside of San Francisco, California, with her husband, Andrea, daughter, Vanessa, and two cats, Luiso and Winter.

You can visit Alexandra Boiger online at
alexandraboiger.com
on follow her on Instagram
@alexandra_boiger

Don't miss the rest of the books in the

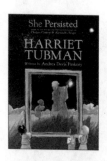
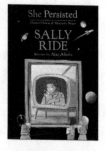
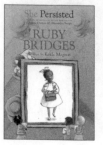

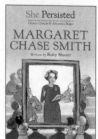

She Persisted series!

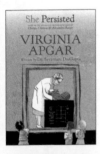

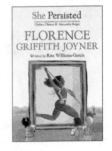

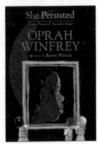